BRYAN LEE O'MALLEY'S

SCOTT PILGRIM
& the infinite
sadness

Production by Steven Birch @ Servo Graphics | edited by James Lucas Jones

Published by Fourth Estate

Originally published in 2006 in the United States by Oni Press

First published in Great Britain in 2010 by
Fourth Estate
An imprint of HarperCollins*Publishers*
1 London Bridge Street
London SE1 9GF
www.4thestate.co.uk

ISBN 978 0 00 793081 4

Printed and bound by CPI Group (UK) Ltd, Croydon, CR0 4YY

www.4thestate.com

DECENT SHOW, EH? TOLD YOU THEY WERE GOOD.

I THINK I'M GONNA THROW UP.

12

i envy you

WH... WHAT IS THAT?

WHAT?

THAT GLOWY THING BY THE DOOR.

HUH... I DON'T KNOW.

WHAT ARE YOU TALKING ABOUT?

THAT, UH, THING?

I THINK IT'S A SAVE POINT.

IT'S A SAVE POINT.

WHAT? ARE YOU SERIOUS?

I GOTTA SAVE BEFORE SHE--

WHAT THE HELL?! YOU'RE NOT SUPPOSED TO BE HERE! WE'RE CLOSED!

UH... WE'RE... WE'RE WITH--

HEY.

backstage

-GLANCE

HI, SCOTT.

SHUT

WHY WERE THEY EVEN *HERE?*

UH... THAT WAS STEPH'S BROTHER, REMEMBER? YOU KNOW HIM.

WAIT... THAT WAS *NEIL?* OH MAN! HA HA... WHOOPS!

I GUESS HE'S DATING THE WRONG GIRL.

I THINK WE SHOULD GET OUT OF HERE.

GIVE ME A SECOND... MY LIFE IS FLASHING BEFORE MY EYES.

1. SCOTT PILGRIM (23 years old)
wants to wake up and realize it was all a crazy dream

2. RAMONA FLOWERS (age unknown)
wants to get the hell out of here ASAP

3. KIM PINE (23 years old)
wants everyone to forget that she dated Scott in high school

4. LYNETTE GUYCOTT (age unknown)
wants to blend into the wall like an awesome ninja

5. STEPHEN STILLS (22 years old)
wants a damn burrito, damn it

I LIKE YOUR OUTFIT, BY THE WAY, RAMONA.

AFFORDABLE?

EXCUSE ME?

I WAS GOING TO SAY, ENVY, DID YOU GET THOSE JEANS IN NEW YORK? THEY'RE TOTALLY—

I'M TALKING TO RAMONA RIGHT NOW.

!

!

RAMONA IS FROM NEW YORK.

MUST STAY IN CONVERSATION AT ALL COSTS →

13 it's only divine right

TODD'S A VEGAN.

IT'S NOT A BIG DEAL.

NO KIDDING! I MEAN, ANYONE CAN BECOME A VEGAN IF THEY WORK AT IT, RIGHT?

UM, NO.

NO. OVO-LACTO VEGETARIAN, MAYBE.

UH... WHY NOT?

MOST PEOPLE JUST CAN'T TAKE IT. IT'S A FACT OF SCIENCE. THE MAIN THING TO KNOW IS THAT I'M BETTER THAN MOST PEOPLE.

UH... HEY.

HOW DOES NOT EATING DAIRY PRODUCTS GIVE YOU PSYCHIC POWERS, ANYWAY? I'VE BEEN WONDERING.

YOU KNOW HOW YOU ONLY USE TEN PERCENT OF YOUR BRAIN?

THIS IS ANOTHER FACT OF SCIENCE?

WELL, IT'S BECAUSE THE OTHER 90 PERCENT IS FILLED UP WITH CURDS AND WHEY!

THAT'S THE STUPIDEST THING I EVER HEARD!!

MAYBE IF YOU KNEW THE SCIENCE...

ANYWAY, THAT'S WHY YOU CAN'T WIN THIS FIGHT, SCOTT, AND YOU'LL HAVE TO GIVE UP ON DATING THIS GIRL.

YEAH... I DON'T THINK IT'S STOPPING ANYTIME SOON.

I'LL SEE YOU GUYS AT BAND PRACTICE.

YOU'RE NOT COMING TO THE THING? THE HONEST ED'S THING?

BLOW ME.

WAS THAT AWKWARD? IS SHE PISSED?

WELL... SEE YOU TOMORROW OR WHATEVER

SO YOU'RE SAYING I SHOULD STAY OVER AT RAMONA'S?

UH...

DON'T I KNOW IT.

RAMONA, PLEEEEASE... I PICKED UP THIS BOY AND WE ONLY HAVE ONE BED IN OUR APARTMENT AND I NEED THE ONE BED FOR THE CUDDLING!

RAMONA, I LOVE YOU. I'LL LOVE YOU FOREVER. AND I HAVE DIPPING SAUCE FOR YOU! I'LL BE YOUR DIPPING SAUCE BITCH!

DUDE, IT'S OKAY. SCOTT CAN COME OVER. HE JUST... HE... HE SMELLS LIKE TRASH.

BUT IT'S OKAY.

I'M JUST TIRED AND CRANKY AND LIKE... HOW DID HE DATE HER? WHAT'S WRONG WITH HIM?!

LET'S BE FRIENDS BASED ON MUTUAL HATE.

IT'S UNREAL.

LOOK AT HIM! HE'S SO CUTESY AND UNASSUMING.

CUTESY?

OH HEY, SCOTT, GIVE ME YOUR KEYS. I FORGOT MY KEYS.

14
about to
e-x-p-l-o-d-e

SCOTT...

SCOTT!

GOOD MORNING, SCOTT!

COME ON, SLEEPYHEAD! UP AND AT 'EM!

I BROUGHT YOU A DOUBLE DOUBLE AND A SOUR CREAM GLAZED.

DUH...

I WAS JUST WALKING MOBILE TO THE BUS STOP. WHAT ARE YOU DOING HERE SO EARLY? IT'S NOT EVEN NINE.

I GOT UP REALLY EARLY AND I THOUGHT I WAS WIDE AWAKE BUT I WASN'T.

AND I FORGOT YOU HAD MY KEY.

AWW, POOR WIDDLE BABY!

I'M SOAKING WET.

HANG ON, I'LL SHOW YOU A TRICK MOBILE TAUGHT ME LAST NIGHT.

EW, WHAT?

NO, IT'S... YOU KNOW YOUR CHI? THINK ABOUT SPREADING YOUR CHI ALL OVER THE SURFACE OF YOUR BODY, AND THEN, UM, YOU KIND OF—

SSHHHAAAAA

WHAT? CHI? WHAT?

IS THIS ONE OF YOUR GAY CHAKRA TANTRIC SPECIAL ABILITIES OR WHATEVER?

DRY ▶

NO, IT'S A PSYCHIC THING. MOBILE IS PSYCHIC.

SU

and then, honest ed's imploded.

SALMON IKURA DON

KISSING
SOUNDS

UM... LET'S STOP.

CAN WE STOP?

STOP WHAT?

GOD, I FEEL WEIRD... I'M TOTALLY NOT EVEN HERE.

WHERE AM I? WHERE ARE YOU, SCOTT?

I JUST KEEP PICTURING ENVY'S STUPID FACE AND GETTING ALL TURNED OFF.

I THINK I'M HAVING THE OPPOSITE PROBLEM.

FLICK

THIS IS SO STUPID.

YEAH, SO... I DUNNO... WE LIKED EACH OTHER?

IT WAS JUST... YEAH... IT WAS HIGH SCHOOL. IT WAS COOL, I GUESS.

THAT'S IT?

YEAH, I MOVED. I MOVED HERE. IT KIND OF ENDED. WE CHANGED.

THAT'S IT?!

WHAT DO YOU WANT?

OKAY! I HAD TO FIGHT A DUDE TO GET WITH HER! I FOUGHT A CRAZY SEVEN-FOOT-TALL PURPLE-SUITED DUDE! AND I HAD TO FIGHT 96 GUYS TO GET TO HIM, TOO!

HE WAS FLYING AND SHOOTING LIGHTNING BOLTS FROM HIS EYES AND HE COULD MAKE PEOPLE DO WHATEVER HE SAID AUTOMATICALLY! HE WAS TOTALLY AWESOME! AND I KICKED HIM SO FAR HE SAW THE CURVATURE OF THE EARTH!!

OKAY, SHUT UP NOW. I'M GOING TO BED.

WHY ARE YOU SO INTERESTED IN KIM, ANYWAY?

WHAT? I DON'T KNOW...

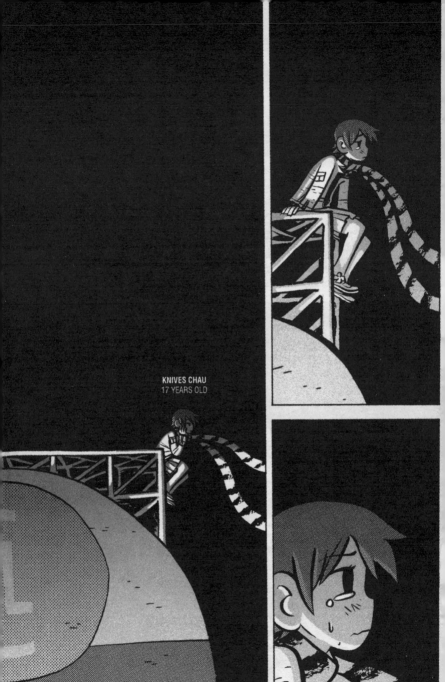

KNIVES CHAU
17 YEARS OLD

16

frail &
bedazzled

YOU KNOW WHAT? I'M A ROCK STAR. I DO WHAT I WANT.

IT'S JUST ONCE IN A WHILE, YOU KNOW? I'M GONNA LIVE A LITTLE. IT'S NOT HURTING ANYONE! AND WHO'S GONNA KNOW?

YOU'RE INCORRIGIBLE.

I DON'T KNOW THE MEANING OF THE WORD.

(he really doesn't)

KISS

DRAMATIC MUSIC IS PLAYING RIGHT NOW

time

SO DID ENVY EVER—

OKAY, WAIT, CAN WE STOP USING HER PRECIOUS LITTLE NICKNAME?

WHAT'S HER ACTUAL NAME?

passed

DUDE?

ARE YOU IN HERE?

HHRRUUGGHHK

DON'T COME OVER HERE!!

WHAT?? AWW, DUDE, YOU'RE ACTUALLY PUKING?!

CHBLLEGGHH

SHUT UP! IT'S NOT MY FAULT!

-HLK-

H... HAVE YOU SEEN JULIE?

WHAT? JULIE? NO. WHAT? I DON'T CARE. I CAN'T BELIEVE YOU'RE PUKING!

CAN YOU FIND HER? I THINK SHE'S MAD AT ME.

BLRRGHH

WHATEVER! HAVE FUN THROWING UP, DICK!

I'LL CATCH YOU LATER ON!

lee's palace
that night

Julie

HEY, IS STEPHEN STILL IN THE BATHROOM VOMITING?

HEY! COOL! YEP! FINE! I GOTTA GO!

HEY... AREN'T YOU SCOTT PILGRIM?

N-NO! I DON'T KNOW!

nubile asian teens

...

?

SCOTT!

OH, HEY, GUYS...

GOOD EVENING,

Wallace Wells gay roommate low moral fibre

Stacey Pilgrim Scott's kid sister rarin' to go

Michael Comeau knows everyone including you

HEY, BRO.

'SUP, SCOTT.

YOU GUYS ARE HERE SO EARLY!

YEAH, WE THOUGHT WE'D GET A HEAD START ON THE DRINKING.

HEY, SCOTT, DID YOU KNOW THAT I HATE HER? ENVY ADAMS? I HATE HER.

I DID NOT KNOW THAT!

DUDE, I'M SO SERIOUS.

HEY SCOTTY, CHECK OUT MY RING.

SSSCOTTTT...

Hollie
works at a video store with Kim

Joseph
Hollie's gay roommate

YO.

YOU GUYS CAME TO SEE THESE ASSHOLES *TWICE??*

UH... NO, WE CAME TO SEE *YOU.*

I PUT THEM ON OUR GUESTLIST, DOOF.

I CAME FOR TODD INGRAM AND TODD INGRAM ALONE.

I USED TO DATE HIM.

OKAY, TALK AMONGST YOURSELVES. I GOTTA GO CHECK ON STEPHEN STILLS.

HE'S IN THE BATHROOM THROWING UP, CAN YOU BELIEVE IT?

YES.

HEY,
SCOTT.

HEY!
ENVY!
H–HI!

HEY,
I HAD
AN
IDEA.

WHAT
WAS
THAT?

I
THOUGHT
MAYBE WE
COULD TALK
LIKE
NORMAL
PEOPLE.

LIKE IT
USED
TO BE.

HOW
CAN I TALK
TO YOU LIKE
A NORMAL
PERSON?
LOOK AT
YOU!

Cheese Dairy

H MY OD, NVY AMS!

ENVY!

ENVY, TALK TO ME!

YOU GN CD?

ENVY ADAMS IS RIGHT THERE!

SO HOT!

RIGGEST AN!

NVY! NVY!!

ELIEVE HE'S HERE!

GOD!

BY HEART!

I LOVE YOU!

T HERE!

YO ROC

NVY DAMS!

KNIVES CHAU
17 YEARS OLD

SKRTCH SKRTCH

UM... HEY, KNIVES.

QUAY CUR

SCOTT!

YEAH...

OKAY, CANADIANS ARE OFFICIALLY BORING PEOPLE.

I TOLD YOU I DIDN'T WANT TO TALK ABOUT IT! IT'S ANCIENT HISTORY.

I MOVED DOWN HERE LAST YEAR AND SCOTT WAS...

...WELL, EXACTLY THE SAME, BUT COMPLETELY DIFFERENT. YOU KNOW? SOMETHING HAPPENED TO HIM. ENVY ADAMS, I GUESS.

THAT UNBELIEVABLE BITCH.

?

HEY, WHAT'S EVERY-BODY—

ENVY, ARE YOU THERE? COME ON, PICK UP.
WELL, I WAS JUST, UH... I WAS JUST THINKING ABOUT YOU, AND I THOUGHT I'D TRY CALLING.
BUT, UH, I GUESS I'LL TRY AGAIN LATER.
ING
RIIING
RIIIING
CLICK
WH- WHAT WAS THAT? WHO IS THAT?
OH... GOD... IT'S THIS GUY JACOB...
HE CALLS SOMETIMES...
DID YOU USED TO DATE HIM OR SOMETHING?
SORT OF... NOT REALLY...
ARE YOU...
...CHEATING ON ME?

OH MY GOD
OH MY GOD

ENVY'S GONNA
SMUSH THEM

ENVY'S CRAZY!
SHE BROKE MY HEART!!
I GOTTA... I GOTTA
DO SOMETHING!!!

BUT WHAT CAN I—

YEAH!
I KNOW!

I GOTTA
BELIEVE!!

they were eleven

Once upon a time, there was a boy and a girl. They lived as next-door neighbours in a small town called Montreal, and their love was as pure as pure can be.

But it was not to last. One day, the boy and his family moved away to a distant land of mountains and dairy cows. The girl grew up alone, and never found another she could truly love, though she tried her hardest.

GRADUATION

Aₙₐ then, at last, when all seemed lost, the boy returned.

Promising they would never again part, the boy displayed his affection in a most remarkable and *unprecedented* fashion...

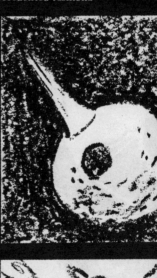

so then todd came back...

blink
blink =

SO... UH... WHAT'D I MISS?

SHOVE

WHOSE ARE THEY?!

WHA?

THE PANTIES ON YOUR HEAD!!

OH, UM...

HOW DID THAT HAPPEN? THAT'S CRAZY!

YOU! RIGHT UNDER MY NOSE THIS WHOLE TIME?! YOU'RE SO FIRED!

SHF

SWING

WHATEVER! SAYONARA, SUCKERS!!

ENVY!! SHE'S TELEPORTING!!

SHE CAN TRY!

THAT'S NOT ALL YOU WON'T BE DOING!! GOD, YOU ASSHOLE...

C'MON, BABY, SHE MEANT NOTHING TO ME. IT'S JUST A THING IN THE PAST.

ENVY... YOU'RE MY GIRL.

OH, TODD...

LET'S BOTH BE GIRLS!!

HRRGGHHH

TWUNK

N-NO WAY! TODD'S WEAK POINT IS... HIS NUTS?!

THAT'S GOTTA HURT!!

SHAAAAAA

18

destroy all vegans

I THINK IT'S TIME TO END THIS VOLUME.

OH, IT'S ON, PILGRIM. YOU'RE GOING DOWN...

BASS BATTLE: FIGHT!!

INCREDIBLE BASS SOLO

HE'S... GOOD!

UH-OH.

THAT'S RIGHT, PILGRIM... I ACTUALLY KNOW HOW TO PLAY BASS.

WE ARE SEX BOB-OMB! ONE TWO THREE FOUR!!

OH MY GOD, I HOPE THEY HAVE A CD! AND THE SINGER WAS HOT!

EW, YOU THINK SO?

WELL, THEY'RE NO CLASH AT DEMONHEAD, THAT'S FOR SURE.

ENH.

DID YOU LIKE IT?

I'M NOT SURE. I NEED SOME TIME TO THINK ABOUT IT.

the decembeR

THEY PROBABLY DON'T SUCK TOO BAD, BUT THE LEVELS WERE HORRIBLE.

ALSO, TODD INGRAM IS A DICK, AND HE ISN'T THAT HOT. YES HE IS

YOU KNOW WHAT? KEEP FILMING, I DON'T EVEN CARE! I HATE THIS STUPID BAR. I'M QUITTING ON MONDAY!

ANY THOUGHTS ON TONIGHT'S EVENTS?

SIP

I wasn't sure what direction to take with the Vegan Police, so I asked my friend Nathan Avery to help me out. These are his original designs. I chickened out and simplified them a lot, but the spirit is there.

BONUS SECTION

I THOUGHT IT WOULD BE NICE (OR AT LEAST INTERESTING) TO ASK SOME FRIENDS TO CONTRIBUTE A FEW LITTLE THINGS FOR THE BACK OF THE BOOK, AND HOPEFULLY I CAN GET A FEW MORE THINGS FOR THE NEXT BOOK. THE IDEA IS THAT IT'S FUN FOR THEM (THE CREATORS) AND YOU (THE READERS) AND WE ALL GET TO SEE DIFFERENT INTERPRETATIONS OF THE CHARACTERS OR WHATEVER. ANYWAY, PLEASE ENJOY.

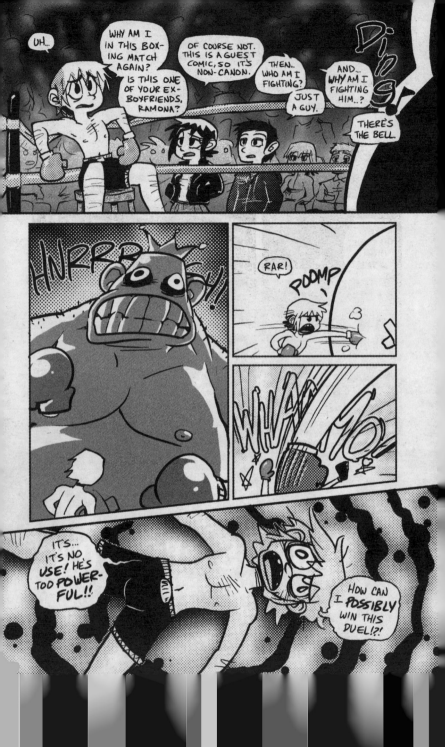

"SCOTT PILGRIM VS. KING HIPPO".
by josh l.

JOHN ALLISON draws the delightfully English webcomic **Scary Go Round** *(www.scarygoround.com)*. I admire him for his ability to draw fashion and to change his characters' hairstyles at will, which I strive to emulate.

ABOUT THE AUTHOR Bryan Lee O'Malley *(born 21 February 1979)* is a Canadian cartoonist and occasional musician. He lives in the wilderness with Hope Larson (**www.hopelarson.com**) and three cats, and has an extremely great website at **www.radiomaru.com**.

this is kind of like a blog

I got re-obsessed with manga while I was working on this book. Here's some stuff that I can remember reading, in no particular order, that I more or less recommend: **BERSERK** (Kentaro Miura), **GANTZ** (Hiroya Oku), **DEATH NOTE** (Tsugumi Ohba & Takeshi Obata), **AZUMANGA DAIOH** (Kiyohiko Azuma), **LIVING GAME** (Mochiru Hoshisato). There's a lot of good stuff out there if you can get past the fanboy/fangirling...

Some people have been asking about the music I listen to while working on Scott Pilgrim. For each book, I tend to make one mix CD of songs that capture the right mood. I don't have much space here, so I'll just list a few major songs...

PLUMTREE - "Scott Pilgrim" - this is the song that inspired the book in general, by a great Canadian indie girl-rock band from the 90s. Plumtree rocks forever!

JOEL PLASKETT - "When I Have My Vision", "Written All Over Me", etc - he's a guy whose music has had a huge influence on me and Scott Pilgrim. He was also in a great 90s band called Thrush Hermit whose defining album "Clayton Park" is an overlooked classic.

THE FLYING BURRITO BROS - "To Ramona", etc - this legendary band fronted by Gram Parsons in the early 70s is the soundtrack to Scott's mind.

BEACHWOOD SPARKS - "By Your Side" - a swirly cosmic countrified cover of a Sade song. It's the ultimate Scott Pilgrim love song. I secretly love the original, too.

THE REPLACEMENTS - "Left of the Dial", "Can't Hardly Wait", etc - they wrote amazing songs. I always think of them as Ramona's favorite band. They're one of mine.

UNCLE TUPELO - "Grindstone" - the original alt-country band. I equate them with the character Stephen Stills.

NEIL YOUNG - "Borrowed Tune" - and every other Neil Young song. Scott also 'borrowed' a tune from the Rolling Stones in this book, in case you missed it...

SPOON - "Waiting For The Kid To Come Out" - gets me moving every time. This is an old b-side but it screams Scott Pilgrim to me. Rockin' and ramshackle.

OLD 97s - "Let The Idiot Speak", etc - they're a bouncy pop-country-punk-something band from Texas and they've given this comic a lot of juice over the years.

TOM PETTY - "American Girl" - this song plays over the credits of every episode of Scott Pilgrim in my mind. Check out that guitar in the intro! *CLASSIC ROCK!*

REMEMBER VOLUMES 1 & 2?

No? Let's see if I can... okay, **Scott** was dating **Knives**, and everyone made fun of him for it. He was having dreams about **Ramona**, who he'd never met, and then he saw her in real life, became obsessed and eventually asked her out. She has **seven evil ex-boyfriends** and Scott has to defeat them all in order to keep dating her. So far he's beaten two of them! The third one is **Todd**, who happens to be dating Scott's ex, **Envy Adams**. They're in a band called **The Clash At Demonhead**, and Scott's band **Sex Bob-omb** is supposed to open for them on **Sunday** (that's in two days!). Meanwhile, Knives is suddenly dating **Neil** (presumably to make Scott jealous), **Stephen Stills** is insanely nervous about the show, **Kim** is feeling weird about meeting Envy, and Scott is freaking out too (he isn't over her!). Time's up! Turn to page 1!!!